# Contents

Mr. WILLIAM

# SHAKESPEARES

COMEDIES,
HISTORIES, &
TRAGEDIES.

Published according to the True Originall Copies.

Martin Droeshout sculpsit London.

*LONDON*
Printed by Isaac Iaggard, and Ed. Blount. 1623.

# SHAKESPEARE
## A LITERARY CHALLENGE

## Helen Barton

BartonBooks

First published in 2009 by BartonBooks

# BartonBooks

Copyright © Helen Barton 2009

ISBN    978-0-9527257-7-0

Typeset and designed by Bookcraft, Stroud, Gloucestershire
Printed and bound in the UK by The Dorset Press, Dorchester

# Introduction

Amidst our current obsession with brand names, icons and images, the picture on the page opposite surely remains one of the most recognisable – William Shakespeare, born over four hundred years ago in a small English midland town whose name will forever be associated with him. There is a constant and continual pilgrimage to Stratford, and Globe Theatres can be found in London, Washington, Tokyo and beyond. Shakespeare continues to be taught in schools and colleges, his plays are read, studied, performed, translated and adapted for film and television. The undertaking by the RSC to perform the cycle of all 37 plays in a year involved a truly global and diverse cast of performances, from small Cornish theatre companies to Brazilian, Indian and Japanese productions. Shakespeare's life has been, and continues to be, meticulously researched, analysed and documented.

Yet despite the fascination and the research, the dissection and the analysis, Shakespeare retains more than an element of mystery. 'It is a great comfort … that so little is known concerning the poet. The life of William Shakespeare is a fine mystery and I tremble every day lest something should turn up.' So says Charles Dickens. The 'dark lady' of the sonnets, the 'unknown' or 'lost' years, even the actual date of his birth, continue to be open to conjecture and interpretation. Was Shakespeare Italian? There is a hypothesis to allege that he was. This, although not a widely supported view, would clearly go a considerable way to explaining his knowledge of Italian.

'I no longer believe that William Shakespeare the actor from Stratford was the author of the works that have been ascribed to him.' So says … who? The answer may be found inside this book. The authorship of the plays has been widely debated – did Shakespeare really write them or was it the Earl of Oxford, Christopher Marlowe or even Francis Bacon? And this despite the fact that his name, typed into research engines, brings up page after page of documentation, commentary and annotation, all of which appears to make him instantly accessible. There are facts and figures on the Bard, most frequently asked questions, bibliographies and timelines, chronologies and forums, summaries, debates and quotations.

I came to compile this book (together with its companion volume on Austen) almost by chance. After an M.A. in English Renaissance Poetry, work in a London publishing house and a move with my family to Worcester, twenty miles from Stratford-upon-Avon, I decided to compile a quiz book on Shakespeare. Literally self-published from the kitchen table, and road-tested on my children (who confused *Hamlet* with 'omelette' and *The Tempest* with *The Temple of Doom*), *The Shakespeare Quiz Book* was followed by companion titles on Austen, Dickens and the Brönte sisters.

*Shakespeare's funerary monument in Holy Trinity Church, Stratford-upon-Avon, created by Gerard Johnson the Younger, c. 1616.*

*Shakespeare's tomb and memorial in a 1910 painting by E. W. Haslehust, published by Blackie and Son in Shakespeareland.*

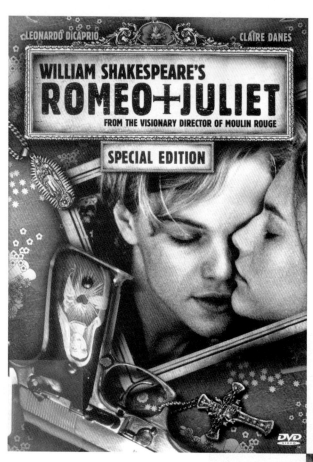

*DVD cover for a film adaptation of Romeo and Juliet.*

*Henry V 1944 film adaptation, starring Lawrence Olivier.*

*Shakespeare: A Literary Challenge* was subsequently compiled and published to include pictures, photographs and graphics, as well as sections dedicated to specific plays. It is intended to have a broad appeal: Shakespeare and theatre fans are not the sole audience. Families and students, teachers, librarians, book groups, those who belong to quiz teams and those who don't – all are invited to use and enjoy this book. Questions are graded from easy, via medium and difficult, to those requiring research. The answers are given separately at the back.

Inside, you will therefore find picture questions, multiple choice questions, and questions which simply require a true or false answer alongside those which present more of a challenge. Film enthusiasts will be tested on their knowledge of television and film adaptations while those well versed in *Hamlet, Macbeth, A Midsummer Night's Dream* or *Romeo and Juliet* will find individual sections on each of these plays. General sections such as 'Deaths, Ghosts and Gory Bits' and 'Identify the Play' are also included.

The intention of this book is to provide the reader with an entertaining approach to Shakespeare, his life and the plays. The reader may be accomplished in all things Shakespearian, keen to test her or his knowledge. On the other hand, he or she may be a fledgling student, requiring informal and lighthearted revision. Those who are entertained by the more eccentric question may appreciate the one concerning the connection between Shakespeare and the import of starlings into America.

When I gave my daughter, then aged three, a copy of the first edition, she asked rather unenthusiastically: 'Do I have to open it?' I hope that none of you say the same thing. And finally ... reading this introduction may prove useful when it comes to answering some of the questions!

# Shakespeare, his Family, his Life and Times

1 Where was Shakespeare born?

2 What is remarkable about the date of his death?

3 Shakespeare had twins. True or false?

4 Which of these is correct? His wife was called:
(a) Elizabeth
(b) Anne
(c) Mary

5 Was she:
(a) older
(b) younger
(c) the same age as him?

6 Shakespeare is often known by another name. What is it?

7 Identify this woman.

8 What was the religion of Mary Arden's family?

9 Which of Shakespeare's works is connected to the Dark Lady?

10 Complete these titles:
(a) *Titus* ...
(b) *Love's* ... ...
(c) *All's* ... ... ... ...
(d) *Much* ... ... ...

11 How many sonnets did Shakespeare write?
Was it:
(a) 134
(b) 144
(c) 154?

12 How is Gilbert Shakespeare connected to William?

# Shakespeare, his Family, his Life and Times

1 Where in Stratford is Shakespeare thought to have been born?

2 Name both of Shakespeare's parents.

3 What was his father's profession?

4 Where would you find the picture below?

5 J. T. are his initials. Who is he and how is he connected to the painting?

6 Which school is Shakespeare thought to have attended?

7 What is the relevance of Snitterfield to Shakespeare's family?

8 Towards the end of 1594, Shakespeare belonged to a playing company. Which three roles did he have with them?

9 What was the playing company called and why was this their name?

10 His initials are C. M. and this is thought to be his portrait. Who is he?

11 Name the two poems by Shakespeare whose initials are V and A and ALC?

# Shakespeare, his Family, his Life and Times

1 Give the exact date of Shakespeare's baptism.

2 Why is this date of particular relevance?

3 Shakspere, Shaksper, Shazper and Shake-speare. Explain.

4 An earlier question (6 Medium) refers to Shakespeare's assumed school. Why exactly is it presumed that he attended this particular school?

5 26 May 1583 and 2 Feburary 1585.
What is significant about these dates?

6 What are the 'lost years' and when were they?

7 Identify the person below and connect him to Shakespeare.

8   What is this?

9   Nathan Field, George Bryan and Joseph Taylor. Who are they?

10   Connect Francis Collins to Shakespeare.

11   'Shine forth, thou Starre of Poets, and with rage,
Or influence, chide, or cheere the drooping Stage;
Which, since thy flight from hence, hath mourn'd like night,
And despaires day, but for thy Volumes light.'

These lines were written in memory of Shakespeare by whom?

12   Susanna, Shakespeare's daughter, had a child called Elizabeth. Who did Elizabeth marry?

13   Whose signature is this?

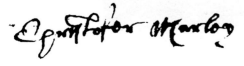

# Shakespeare, his Family, his Life and Times

1 The clues are 3 May and the Gregorian calendar. What is the answer?

2 'an upstart crow, beautified with our feathers, that with his *Tygers hart wrapt in a Players hyde,*' Who said this about Shakespeare?

3 See the italicised part of the above question and explain its significance.

4 In 1599, an anthology of poetry was published and was initially attributed to Shakespeare. What was it called and how many of the poems did Shakespeare actually write?

5 *The Rape of Lucrece* and *Venus and Adonis* were both dedicated to the same person. Who was he?

6 E. de V., F. B. Whose initials are these and what is their significance to Shakespeare?

7 What is the association between Gerard Johnson and Shakespeare?

8   Shakespeare's sonnets, published in 1609, contained all but two of the poems. Which two were missing and why?

9   An earlier question (4 Medium) referred to a painting. Answer the following questions on this same picture.
(a) What is this portrait known as and why?
(b) At one point, the portrait was owned by William Davenant. Who was he?

10   £13 3s 6d is the clue. What is the answer?

11   What is the connection between Shakespeare and a Spanish writer of the same period?

# Locations, Buildings and Settings

1 Where is Shakespeare buried?

2 Name two plays that have Venice as their setting.

3 Locate the picture below and say what it is.

4 How many gentlemen are there in the play with Verona in its title?

5 'A ship at sea; afterwards an uninhabited island.' What is the play?

6 Where is *Macbeth* set?

7 'The Roman Empire.' This is the setting for Julius Caesar. True or false?

8   Whose cottage is shown in the photos below?

9   Complete this title: *The Merry Wives of …*

10   What is this?

# Locations, Buildings and Settings

1 Who is said to have come from Temple Grafton?

2 Where would you find the statue shown below?

3 Which play is set in Vienna?

4 Where would you find this?

5  Where is Pericles from?

6  What building is shown below, where is it and who is the architect?

# Locations, Buildings and Settings

**7** 'A city in Illyria; and the sea-coast near it.' What is the play?

**8** What is the setting for
*The Taming of the Shrew*?

**9** Look at the picture below. Where would you find it and what is it?

10 Apart from the Forest of Arden, *As You Like It* has two other locations. What are they?

11 One of the settings in this play is Bohemia. The flag below is of its other location. What is the location and what is the play?

12 Which two plays have locations that are almost identical, in that they are both set in Athens and a wood?

# *Locations, Buildings and Settings*

1 Make the connection between this flag and a setting and you will have the name of the play.

2 St Saviour's Church, Southwark is his burial place. Who is he?

3 In which country would you find the Globe Theatre shown below?

4 Give the four locations of *All's Well That Ends Well*.

5  Below are three pictures of Globe Theatres in America.
In which states would you find them?

(a)

(b)

(c)

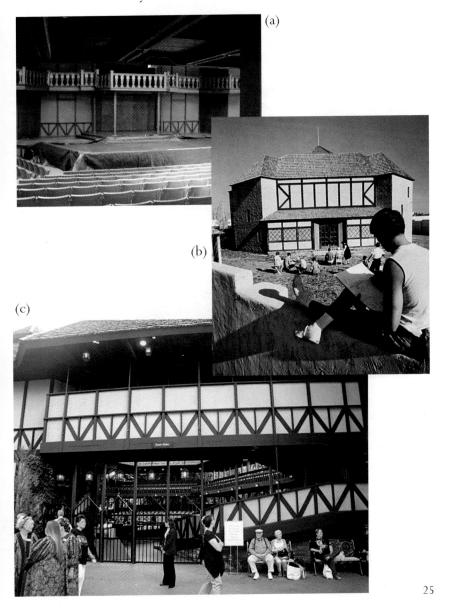

25

# *Locations, Buildings and Settings*

6 Connect this picture with Shakespeare.

7 Seven plays have locations in their (full) titles. Name as many of them as you can.

8  Whose house is this and where would you find it?

9  Kimbolton, Epheseus and 'Dispersedly in various countries' are the settings, but can you name the plays?

10  The number 23 and the picture below are the clues. What is the answer?

11  *Julius Caesar* has three locations. Rome is one. What are the other two?

# *Locations, Buildings and Settings*

1 In 1596, where was Shakespeare living? Be as precise as you can.

2 If you can make this connection, you will have a setting for one of the tragedies.

3 If Hugh Clopton is the clue, which building is the answer?

4 How much did Shakespeare pay for New Place and what was unusual about it?

5 Shakespeare bought a property in London – if you can identify the location of the picture below you will have the answer.

6   Whose house is shown below and what is its connection to Shakespeare?

# Locations, Buildings and Settings

7 Give the three settings of *Coriolanus*.

8 Name and locate the building shown below and explain the connection to Shakespeare.

9 Look at the picture below.
Give the date and as much description of this building as you can.

10 A mulberry tree and the Reverend Francis Gastrell are the clues to a building. What is it and what is the connection?

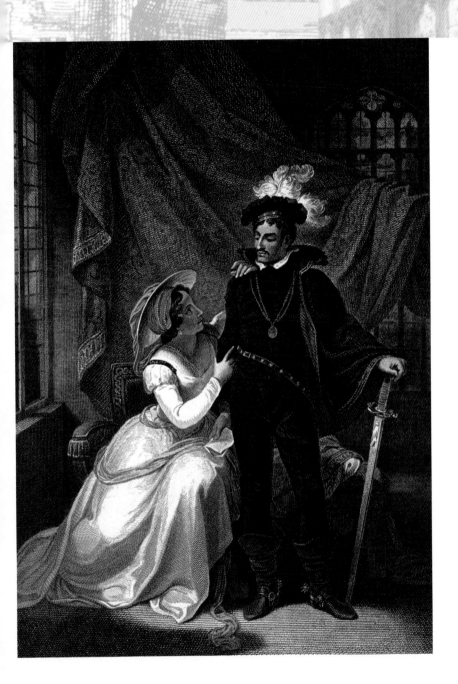

# Deaths, Ghosts and Gory Bits

1 Identify the main character in this picture.

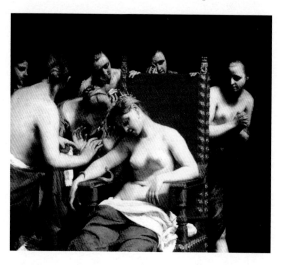

2 Which is considered the most bloodthirsty play and was Shakespeare's first tragedy?

3 In the picture below, who is this?

4 In *Othello* Desdemona is strangled. True or false?

5 How does Cleopatra commit suicide?

6 Ghosts of Richard's victims appear in one of the plays but which one is it?

7 Look at the picture below and identify the ghost and the play.

# Deaths, Ghosts and Gory Bits

8 'O, I am slain! If thou be merciful,
Open the tomb, lay me with Juliet.'
Who is speaking and who has mortally wounded him?

9 Who are the female characters in the picture below?

10 How does Hamlet die?

11 Who kills Macbeth and enters, at the end of the play, with his head?

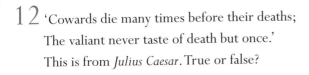

12  'Cowards die many times before their deaths;
     The valiant never taste of death but once.'
     This is from *Julius Caesar*. True or false?

13  '*Enter a* Gentleman *with a bloody knife*.' Where is this from?
     (a) *Titus Andronicus*
     (b) *Coriolanus*
     (c) *King Lear*

14  'this dead butcher, and his fiend-like queen'. Who are they?

15  Identify the two characters in the picture below.

# Deaths, Ghosts and Gory Bits

1 Who dies singing 'Willow, willow, willow.'?

2 Identify the character from the following: 'she fell distract, And, her attendants absent, swallow'd fire.'

3 Who are the two main characters in this picture?

4 In a play, bearing his name, this character serves a mother with a pie containing her dead sons. Who is he?

5 Five suicides take place during the course of one of the plays. Which one is it?

6 Name as many of them as you can.

7 'With all my heart I'll send the Emperor my hand. Good Aaron, wilt thou help to chop it off?' Who is speaking?

8 'I have done the deed.' What is the deed and who is speaking?

9 This is a picture of Caesar's death, but who strikes the first blow and who the last?

10 'No funeral rite, nor man in mourning weed,
    No mournful bell shall ring her burial;
    But throw her forth to beasts and birds to prey.'
Who is she and what is the play?

11 A mother and son are both killed in *Macbeth*. Who are they?

12 Who in *King Lear* is blinded by Regan and Cornwall and later tries
to commit suicide?

13 'juice of cursed hebenon' is the clue.
What is the play and who has killed who?

14 'I think it is the weakness of mine eyes
    That shapes this monstrous apparition.
    It comes upon me. Art thou any thing?'
Identify the speaker and the apparition.

15 Supply the missing name in the following lines:
    'He hath commission from thy wife and me
    To hang ... in the prison, and
    To lay the blame upon her own despair,
    That she fordid herself.'

16 Identify the character who appears in three plays and whose death is
mentioned in *King Henry The Fifth*.

# Deaths, Ghosts and Gory Bits

1 In one of the plays, both the hero and the villain kill their wives. What is the play and who are the characters?

2 Where would you find Abhorson, an executioner?

3 'He's dead, and at the murderer's horse's tail,
   In beastly sort, dragg'd through the shameful field.'
What is the play, who is the speaker and who is dead?

4 What happens to Bassianus's body in *Titus Andronicus*?

5 Questions 5 and 6 in the Medium Section have asked for details of the five suicides that take place in one play. This leaves eleven suicides that occur in other plays. Name as many characters as you can.

6 In the cast list of which play would you find 'A Son *that has killed his father*. A Father *that has killed his son*'?

7 'Your daughter here the princes left for dead.'
Who is she and what is the play?

8 Buried up to his neck in sand and starved to death.
Who is he and who sentences him to death?

9 Apart from Julius Caesar, another character is stabbed by conspirators. Name him and the leader of his killers.

10 'Here lies a wretched corse, of wretched soul bereft.'
Whose epitaph is this?

11 Which character poisons her sister and why?

12 Using the picture, identify whose death is being portrayed. An extra mark if you know the artist.

13 'For God's sake, let us sit upon the ground
And tell sad stories of the death of kings:
How some have been depos'd, some slain in war,
Some haunted by the ghosts they have depos'd,
Some poison'd by their wives, some sleeping kill'd.'
In which play would you find these lines?

14 She is raped, has her tongue cut out and is finally killed by her father. Who is she?

15 Supply the missing words in this quotation from *King Henry The Fourth*, *Part 2*: 'I were better to be eaten to death with a … than to be scoured to nothing with … … ' For an extra point, identify the speaker.

# REQUIRING RESEARCH

## *Deaths, Ghosts and Gory Bits*

1  The clue is a 'malmsey-butt'. From this, find out who was killed, how and by whom.

2  How is the person in this picture connected to a death in *Hamlet*?

3  B is the place of death, E of R are the killer's initials. From this, work out who has killed who and where.

4  'Now die, die, die, die, die.' Identify the play.

5  'O, Harry, thou hast robb'd me of my youth!' Which dying character speaks these words?

6  'Even here she sheathed in her harmless breast
    A harmful knife, that thence her soul unsheathed.'
Where would you find these lines and who is she?

7  'The King, I fear, is poison'd by a monk;
    I left him almost speechless.'
Who is the King and who is speaking?

40

8 'a resolved villain,
  Whose bowels suddenly burst out.'
Who is this and what is his cause of death?

9 The causes of Shakespeare's own death remain a mystery, but to whom
can the following be attributed? 'Shakespeare, Drayton, and Ben Jonson
had a merry meeting and it seems drank too hard, for Shakespeare died of
a fever there contracted.'

10 Following a seizure, which of Shakespeare's contemporaries died
within one or two years of Shakespeare?

11 The picture below is of one of Shakespeare's contemporaries.
(a) Who is he?
(b) What was his profession?
(c) What was unusual about the day he died?

12 '... it strikes a man more dead than a great reckoning in a
little room.' *As You Like It*. Who do some commentators think is being
referred to in this line?

# *Who or What is This?*

1 Who is Ariel?

2 In *King Henry The Sixth, Part 2* who is Margery Jourdain? Is she:
(a) a lady in waiting    (b) a witch    (c) a nurse?

3 Bianca (*Othello*) is in love with Iago. True or false?

4 'But I am constant as the Northern Star,'. Who is speaking?
An extra point if you can quote anything at all from the next two lines.

5 Who wears an asses head?

6 In this picture, which character is portrayed?

7 'But this rough magic
   I here abjure;'
Who is speaking?

8 The following is from *Julius Caesar*. What is the missing word? Is it:
(a) havoc    (b) murder    (c) vengeance?
'Cry … and let slip the dogs of war'.

9 Who or what are the following characters? Match them correctly:
   Charles (*As You Like It*)    Lavache (*All's Well*)    Dogberry (*Much Ado*)
   Constable                     Clown                     Wrestler

**10** The characters on the right of this picture are Rosalind and Touchstone (*As You Like It*). True or false?

**11** Phebe (*As You Like It*) and Mopsa and Dorcas (*The Winter's Tale*) are connected but how? Are they:

(a) servants    (b) shepherdesses    (c) daughters of queens?

**12** Henry Percy is a character who appears in some of the history plays. What is he also known as?

**13** What is the connection between Touchstone (*As You Like It*), Trinculo (*The Tempest*) and Feste (*Twelfth Night*). (A picture in an earlier question may help you.)

**14** 'Touch but my lips with those fair lips of thine;
    Though mine be not so fair, yet are they red—
    The kiss shall be thine own as well as mine.'
From which work are these lines taken? Is it:

(a) *Romeo and Juliet*    (b) one of the sonnets    (c) *Venus and Adonis*?

**15** What is the connection between Rosalind in *As You Like It* and Viola in *Twelfth Night*?

# Who or What is This?

1 In *The Tempest*, who or what is Stephano?

2 Name the man who is in love with Audrey (*As You Like It*).

3 'Shall I compare thee to a summer's day?' Where is this line from? Be as specific as you can, then quote as much as possible from the following three lines.

4 '*a gull'd Venetian gentleman*' (*Othello*). Who is he?

5 Supply the missing name in the following stage directions: *Enter ... alone, in boy's clothes.*

6 Iris, Ceres and Juno. Who are they?

7 The play is *Love's Labour's Lost* and the word is 'honorificabilitudinitatibus' but who is speaking?

8  The following is from *Pericles, Prince of Tyre*.
What are the missing words?
Clues: the first is a type of snake; the second rhymes with feed;
the third and fourth are members of the family.
>'I am no ... , yet I feed
>On mother's flesh which did me ...
>I sought a ... , in which labour
>I found that kindness in a ... :
>He's father, son, and husband mild;
>I mother, wife, and yet his child.
>How they may be, and yet in two,
>As you will live, resolve it you.'

9  In *Timon of Athens*, four minor characters are simply described by their
occupations. What are they?

10  'green-ey'd monster', one of the many Shakespearian phrases
still in use today.
Who says it to whom?
Quote as many of the relevant lines as possible.

11  Which female character appears in one of the comedies and
three of the histories?

12 Who makes her first appearance in these lines? Locate them as accurately as you can.

> 'In the old age black was not counted fair
> Or if it were, it bore not beauty's name;
> But now is black beauty's successive heir,
> And beauty slandered with a bastard shame;'

13 Who are the two characters in the picture below?

14 What are the missing words in the following lines?

> 'I'll break my ... ,
> Bury it certain ... in the earth,
> And, deeper than did ever ... sound,
> I'll drown my ... '

37.

"Gives not the hawthorne-bush a sweeter shade
To shepherds, looking on their silly sheep,
Than doth a rich embroidered canopy
To kings that fear their subjects' treachery?"

3 Henry VI., Act ii., sc. 5.

# *Who or What is This?*

1 What is the connection between this picture and one of the plays?

2 What thirteen-letter word, beginning with 'a', and with one letter repeated four times, is said to have been invented by Shakespeare. Say exactly where you would find it.

3 The following lines are taken from the St Crispin Day speech (*King Henry The Fifth*):

'Then shall our names,

Familiar in his mouth as household words

..................................................

Be in their flowing cups freshly rememb'red.'

Seven names are mentioned.

How many of them do you know?

4 Who exits 'pursued by a bear'?

5 'Two loves I have, of comfort and despair,
   That like two spirits do suggest me still;
   My better angel is a man right fair,
   My worser spirit a woman colour'd ill.'
From which work are these lines taken?

6 Name the actor in this film adaptation of *King Richard The Third*.

7 What are the next seven lines from this famous speech?
   'Be not afeard; the isle is full of noises,
   Sounds and sweet airs, that give delight and hurt not.
   ....................,'

8   Look at the picture below. What exactly is it?

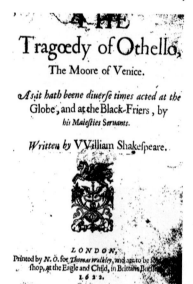

9   There are eight conspirators in *Julius Caesar*. Name as many as you can.

10   The following is from *King Henry the Fourth, Part 1*. Two words in this extract appeared for the first time in the play. What are they?

> 'O, I could divide myself
> and go to buffets, for moving such a dish of
> skim milk with so honourable an action! Hang him!
> let him tell the king: we are prepared. I will set
> forward to-night.'

11  The lines below are taken from
one of the comedies. Which one is it?
'One of these men is
genius to the other;
And so of these:
Which is the natural man,
And which the spirit?'

12  What is Griffith's role in *King Henry The Eighth*?

13  Identify the character in the picture below.

14  *A Midsummer Night's Dream* and *Love's Labour's Lost* have a character
with the same name. Who is it?

15  Who are Helicanus and Escanes?

## *Who or What is This?*

1 Part of his name in French means 'fire' and his age is indicated in the Dramatis Personae. Who is he?

2 The clues are Tennyson, problem and the two plays that each have one word repeated twice in their titles. What is the answer?

3 Name the director of this recent film adaptation of *The Merchant of Venice*.

4 A number, Christmas, a town in Italy and a name associated with lovers. Can you link these together to find the answer?

5 What is the connection between Shakespeare, the bird shown here and the USA?

6 The following are words invented by Shakespeare. In which of his plays do they first occur? *zany, madcap, moonbeam, mountaineer.*

7 In order to answer this question, you will need to make the connection between Droitwich Spa in Worcestershire and the First Folio.

8 Below are six signatures by Shakespeare. Say when each of them was used and in what context.

# *Who or What is This?*

9 Which character's original name was Oldcastle?

10 Who promoted this poster?

11 'Small show of man was yet upon his chin;
   His phoenix down began but to appear,
   Like ... ... , on that termless skin,'
Locate this extract and supply the two missing words.

12 He is in *King Richard the Third* and shares a similar profession to
Peter in *Measure for Measure*. Who is he?

13 'The love I dedicate to your Lordship is without end: whereof this
Pamphlet without beginning is but a superfluous Moity.'
Who is the lord and what is the 'Pamphlet'?

14 This picture represents
a scene from one of the tragedies.
Name both the play and
the two characters.

15 Whose signatures are these?

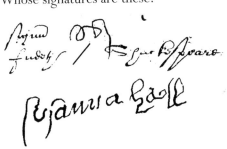

16 What is the significance of the names Morgan, Polydore and Cadwal?

17 'It is a great comfort ... that so little is known concerning the poet.
The life of William Shakespeare is a fine mystery and I tremble every day
lest something should turn up.' Who is speaking?

18 'I no longer believe that William Shakespeare the actor from
Stratford was the author of the works that have been ascribed to him.'
Identify the person who said this.

# Identify the Play

1 Look at the picture below. Is this a film version of:
(a) *A Midsummer Night's Dream*
(b) *Twelfth Night*
(c) *Love's Labour's Lost*?

2 In which play would you find the Montagues and the Capulets?

3 Prospero and Ariel are characters in *The Tempest*. True or false?

4 Valentine and Proteus are the two gentlemen. Name the play.

5 'Now is the winter of our discontent'. Which history play opens with these lines?

6 The King of Sicilia and The King of Bohemia are found in *The Winter's Tale*. True or false?

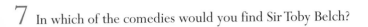

7 In which of the comedies would you find Sir Toby Belch?

8 'Friends, Romans, countrymen, lend me your ears;' Name the play from which these lines are taken.

9 Identify the play from the picture below.

10 In which play would you find the reference to a pound of flesh?

11 Supply the missing word: *Othello, The ... of Venice*

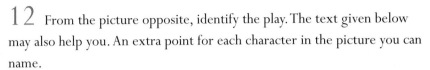

12 From the picture opposite, identify the play. The text given below may also help you. An extra point for each character in the picture you can name.
'O, wonder!
How many goodly creatures are there here!
How beauteous mankind is! O brave new world
That has such people in't!'

13 The play opens with mutinous citizens armed with clubs and other weapons. Is this:
(a) *Julius Caesar*   (b) *Macbeth*   (c) *Coriolanus*?

14 One of the history plays has three parts. Which one is it?

15 What is the full title of *Twelfth Night*?

16 Perdita and Hermione are the characters, but what is the play? Is it:
(a) *The Winter's Tale*   (b) *Measure for Measure*   (c) *Antony and Cleopatra*?

17 Katherine and Bianca are found in *The Taming of the Shrew*. True or false?

18 Match these characters to their plays:
The Prince of Morocco      Elbow and Froth      Cloten
*The Merchant of Venice*      *Measure for Measure*      *Cymbeline*

# *Identify the Play*

1 Helena and Helen are characters who appear in two plays each; Helenus appears in one. What are the plays?

2 'Then must you speak
  Of one that lov'd not wisely, but too well;'
  Identify the play.

3 In which play would you find a character called Adrian?

4 Look at the picture below and name the play.

5 The first two characters to appear on stage are a shipmaster and a boatswain. Identify the play.

6 'La main, de hand; les doigts, de fingers. Je pense que je suis le bon ecolier;' Name the play and the speaker if you can.

7 In which plays does Falstaff appear?

8 Only one play opens with the main character alone on stage. Which one is it?

9 Match these clowns to the plays in which they are found:
Pompey    Launcelot Gobbo

10 How many plays have more than one part to them and what are they?

11 Identify the play in which you would find a Welsh parson and a French physician.

12 Identify the play from this picture.

13 *Before an alehouse on a heath.* This is the opening setting, but what is the play?

14 'The quality of mercy is not strain'd;
    It droppeth as the gentle rain from heaven
    Upon the place beneath.'
Name the play from which
these lines are taken.

15 Look at this picture
and identify the play.

# *Identify the Play*

1 In which play do three female characters all have names that end in 'a'?

2 Juliet appears in another play apart from the obvious one. What is it?

3 'I have a kind of self resides with you.' Where is this from?

4 Firstly, how many plays have the word either 'Prince' or 'King' in their (full) title? Secondly, name them!

5 Eight tragedies are thought to have been written between 1599 and 1608. Name any five of them.

6 'Upon my life, by some device or other
   The villain is o'erraught of all my money.'
Where are these lines taken from?

7 Use the picture below to identify the play.

8 'All the world's a stage,'
Name the play, the speaker and all seven stages of man.

9 Thomas, a friar and Elinor, a queen are characters in two of the plays.
Which ones are they?

10 Can you identify the play from the picture below?

11 Philo opens the play, and a reference to Dolabella closes it. What is it?

12 Caius Lucius is a general of the Roman Forces. In which play would
you find him?

13 Identify all twenty-three eponymous plays.

14 'What's this, what's this? Is this her fault or mine?
    The tempter or the tempted, who sins most?'
Identify the play.

15 Which history play is thought to have been written last?

16 Only one play closes with a female character speaking. Which one is
it?                                                                         63

# *Identify the Play*

1 Use this picture to identify the play.

2 The clues are 29 June 1613 and the Globe Theatre being destroyed by a fire. What is the answer?

3 'I am the Walrus' by the Beatles and BBC Radio 3 are clues. What is the play?

4 Match these characters with their plays:
(a) Melun, a French lord   (b) Ralph Mouldy   (c) Brandon

5 How is this picture connected to one of the plays?

6 'Call forth Bagot.' Identify the play, who exactly is Bagot and where is this particular scene set?

7 Ten of Shakespeare's plays (five comedies, four histories and one tragedy) are thought to have been written between approximately 1594 and 1599. Name as many of them as you can.

8 The picture below is connected to one of the plays. Which one is it?

**9** These are the clues: 1907 is possibly the date of its first recorded performance and 'never staled with the Stage, never clapper-clawd with the palmes of the vulgar' (these lines being taken from its first published edition in 1609). Can you name the play?

**10** Francis Meres mentions this play in his work *Palladis Tamia, Wits Treasury* (1598), but it is thought that it was not staged until John Rich did so in 1745 at Drury Lane. What is it?

**11** Can you name the play that had an eighteenth-century adaptation called *The Sheep-Shearing*.

**12** Look at this picture and identify the play.

**13** R. F., J. F., C. and B. are their initials. Who are they and in which play do they appear?

**14** In which plays are the following characters found:
(a) Vaux    (b) Fang    (c) Sir Stephen Scroop?

"I know a bank where the
          wild thyme blows,—

26.

# *Hamlet*

1 Of which country is Hamlet prince?

2 Match these characters correctly:

Francisco            Marcellus        Fortinbras
Prince of Norway     soldier          officer

3 Polonius has a son and a daughter. True or false?

4 What is Hamlet's relationship to Claudius?

5 Several operas have been written about *Hamlet*, but how many are there?

(a) at least 26    (b) at least 16    (c) at least 36

6 Identify the character in this picture. If you know the artist, you get a bonus point.

7 Whose grave is being dug in the graveyard scene?

8 In 1603, the play was performed at two universities. Which ones were they?

9 July 1601 was the earliest recorded performance of *Hamlet*. True or false?

10 'Something is rotten in the state of Denmark.' This famous line occurs in Act I but who speaks it? (a) Polonius    (b) Hamlet    (c) Marcellus?

11 Claudius plans to send Hamlet abroad, but where? Is it: (a) Norway    (b) Ireland    (c) England?

12 Who kills Hamlet's father and how?

13 Hamlet's father is also called Hamlet. True or false?

# *Hamlet*

1 'Alas, poor Yorick!'
(a) What are the next four words?
(b) Who was Yorick?
(c) Supply the missing words: 'a fellow of infinite ... ,
of most excellent ...'

2 Name as many of the five courtiers as you can.

3 'To be, or not to be – that is the question;'
Quote as much as you can of the next nine lines.

4 What scene is portrayed below?

5 *Rosencrantz and Guildenstern are Dead* and *The Fifteen Minute Hamlet* were both written by the same playwright. Who is he?

6 'his doublet all unbrac'd,
    No hat upon his head, his stocking fouled,
    Ungart'red and down-gyved to his ankle;'
Who is speaking about whom?

7 How is Horatio described in the Dramatis Personae?
Be as precise as you can.

8 What are the circumstances of Gertrude's death?

9 *Self Portrait as Hamlet* was painted in 1821 by a French artist.
Who is he?

10 During the course of the play, Hamlet kills three people on stage.
Name them.

11 What is *The Murder of Gonzago*?

12 In his version of the play in 1772, which two characters did
David Garrick omit?

13 How is Agatha Christie connected to *Hamlet*?

14 The 'bad quarto' or Q1 contains approximately how much of the
text of Q2?

15 His name, when translated from the French, means 'strong arm'.
Who is he?

16 'Neither a borrower nor a lender be;' Who is speaking? Quote as
much as you can from the next two lines.

1 'O, that this too too solid flesh would melt,' Quote as many of the next five lines as you can.

2 Just before she dies, Ophelia makes herself a garland. How many of the four named flowers/plants do you know?

3 Where exactly would you find this?

> *Ham.* **To be, or not to bē, I there's the point,**
> **To Die, to ſleepe, is that all? I all:**
> **No, to ſleepe, to dreame, I mary there it goes,**
> **For in that dreame of death, when wee awake,**
> **And borne before an euerlaſting Iudge,**
> **From whence no paſſenger euer retur'nd,**
> **The vndiſcouered country, at whoſe ſight**
> **The happy ſmile, and the accurſed damn'd.**
> **But for this, the ioyfull hope of this,**
> **Whol'd beare the ſcornes and flattery of the world,**
> **Scorned by the right rich, the rich curſſed of the poore?**

4 *Hamlet* is the longest play. Approximately how many lines and words does it contain?

5 How is this film connected to *Hamlet*?

6 Which nineteenth-century French poet wrote a poem about Ophelia?

7 In Charlie Chaplin's 1957 film *A King in New York*, which character recites the 'To be, or not to be' speech?

8 'the word's of *Hamlet* bring our mind into contact with the eternal wisdom,' Who is speaking?

9 How is the playwright Anton Chekhov connected to *Hamlet*?

**10** 'I believe the character of *Hamlet* may be traced to Shakespeare's deep and accurate science in mental philosophy. Indeed, that this character must have some connection with the common fundamental laws of our nature may be assumed from the fact, that *Hamlet* has been the darling of every country in which the literature of England has been fostered.' This is taken from an essay by a famous English poet. Who is he?

**11** At the start of one of Dickens' novels there is a reference to *Hamlet*. Which one is it?

**12** Where exactly would you find this title page? Date it and whose initials are N. L.?

THE
Tragicall Hist021e of
HAMLET,
*Prince of Denmarke.*

By William Shakefpeare.

Newly imprinted and enlarged to almoft as much againe as it was, according to the true and perfect Coppie.

AT LONDON,
Printed by I. R. for N. I. and are to be fold at his fhoppe vnder Saint Dunftons Church in Fleeftreet. 1605.

**13** Name the actor, director and year of this version.

1 What exactly are the three texts?

2 Odysseus's father. What is the connection?

3 Who is Yorick thought to be based upon?

4 The clue is Corambis. What is the answer?

5 Who is the person below and what is his significance to *Hamlet*?

6 N. R. and L. T. Who were they and what is their connection to *Hamlet*?

7 What does Q1 contain that the others do not?

8 Percy MacKaye wrote four plays as prequels to *Hamlet*. Name as many of them as you can.

9 Which actress has played all these parts: Hamlet, Ophelia and Gertrude?

10 Look at the picture below and answer the following:

(a) who is the actor?

(b) what is the date of the film?

(c) who is the director?

11 This is a picture from a 1992 production. Answer the following:

(a) who was the director?

(b) identify the two actors

(c) who played Ophelia?

12 The clues are: The Dragon, Captain William Keeling and Sierra Leone. What is the answer?

13 'English Seneca read by candle-light yields many good sentences, as Blood is a begger, and so forth; and if you entreat him fair in a frosty morning, he will afford you whole Hamlets, I should say handfuls of tragical speeches.' Who wrote this and when? Where would you find it?

14 What is the ur-Hamlet and how are the initials T K connected to it?

# *Macbeth*

1 What is the opening line of the play?

2 Supply the missing words from the next three lines:
'In thunder, ..., or in ...?
When the ... done,
When the ... lost and ...'

3 When we first see Macbeth, who is he with? Is it:
(a) Lady Macbeth   (b) Banquo   (c) Duncan?

4 Dundee is one of the settings of the play. True or false?

5 'from his mother's womb
   Untimely ripped.'
Who is he and why is this of such significance?

6 Lady Macbeth is first seen in Scene V of the First Act, but what is she doing? Is she:
(a) washing her hands   (b) sleepwalking   (c) reading a letter?

7 Malcolm and Donalbain are Macduff's sons. True or false?

8 Who is this?

9 'Out, damned spot! out, I say!' Who is speaking?

10 Identify the two actors below who appeared in the 1978 version of *Macbeth*.

11 Macbeth is already Thane of Glamis, but the witches make two prophecies when they first meet him. What are they?

12 *Romeo and Juliet* is shorter than *Macbeth*. True or false?

13 How are the three witches otherwise known?

14 In which popular series of childrens' books would you find a rock group called *The Weird Sisters*?

15 Theatrical superstition is attached to *Macbeth* and it is often referred to by another name. What is it?

1 In the Dramatis Personae, how is Macbeth described?

2 There are six noblemen of Scotland. Name as many as you can.

3 By whose death does Macbeth know that he is Thane of Glamis?

4 When Duncan's sons flee, where do they go?

5 In this film version of the play, who played Macbeth?

6 Who directed it?

7 'I will not be afraid of death and bane
Till ...' what?

8 When the play opens, which Scandinavian country has just been defeated?

9 'Is this a dagger which I see before me,' Quote the following two lines.

10 'Here's a knocking indeed!' This is the porter speaking, but who does he open the gate to?

11 Who is Macdonwald?

12 What is the significance of Colmekill?

13 In the following lines, supply the missing word and say who is speaking to whom.

> 'You should be women,
> And yet your ... forbid me to interpret
> That you are so.'

14 What is the first thing that the witches put into the cauldron?

*Macbeth*

1  Newt, frog, dog, blind-worm, lizard and goat are all put into the witches' cauldron. Give the exact part of each one that is added.

2  When Macbeth meets the witches again in Act IV, there are three apparitions. Describe as many of them as you can.

3  The BBC's 2005 series *ShakespeaRe-Told* contained a version of *Macbeth*. Where exactly was this adaptation set and what was Macbeth's profession?

4  King James of Scotland believed he was a descendant of one of the characters in Macbeth, but which one?

5  There is a reference early on in the play to Sweno. Who is he?

6  In Act IV, Macbeth is shown a parade of eight kings. What is the last king holding and what do commentators think that this parade represents?

7  Who wrote *The Sound and The Fury* and what is its connection to Macbeth?

8  Who directed and starred in this film version of *Macbeth*?

9 'And hence, also, there is an entire absence of comedy, nay, even of irony and philosophic contemplation in *Macbeth*,—the play being wholly and purely tragic.' Which poet wrote this?

10 A famous line from *Macbeth* is the title of a novel by Ray Bradbury. What is it?

11 *Macbird*, a 1966 drama by Barbara Garson, featured which American president as *Macbeth*?

12 In the following lines, supply the missing words.
    'I have no spur
    To prick the — of my intent, but
    Vaulting ambition, which — itself,
    And falls on th' other.'

13 This is a self-portrait of an artist who painted a well-known picture of Macbeth and the Three Witches. Who is he?

14 Supply the missing words from the following quotation and say in which Act it occurs. 'Will all great ... ... wash this ... ... from my hand? No, this my hand will rather the ... seas ..., making the ... one ...'

# *Macbeth*

1 How is the person in the picture below connected to *Macbeth*?

2 Some commentators date *Macbeth* as being written between 1605 and 1606. Why?

3 April 1611 and Simon Forman are the clues. What is the answer?

4 'one of the best plays for a stage, and variety of dancing and music, that ever I saw.' Who is speaking and about what?

5 These two people are connected both to each other and to the play: Nikolai Leskov and Dmitri Shostakovich. What is the connection?

6 Link the person in this picture to *Macbeth*.

7 A Scottish philosopher born in the fifteenth century is the clue. Who is he and what is the connection?

8 Who exactly was the real Macbeth, when was he born and how long did he rule?

9 Who directed this version of *Macbeth* and when? What was its English title?

10   *Kumonosu-jô* is the Japanese title. Find the English translation.

11   '*The moon is down*;' Who speaks this line and how is it related to an author whose initials are J. S.?

12   Macbeth's speech '*Ay, in the catalogue ye go for men*;' goes on to list eight types of dog. How many of these can you name? Whose work is thought to be the source of these lines?

13   Who is this and how is he connected to Macbeth?

1   Whose wedding is announced in the opening lines of the play?

2   The wedding is two days away. True or false?

3   Three of the female characters have names beginning with H. Name as many as you can.

4   Robin Goodfellow is better known by another name. What is it?

5   Identify the two characters in this picture.

· AND · I · D° · L♥VE · THEE ·

6   Lysander and Demetrius are both in love with Hermia. True or false?

7   '*Ill met by ..., proud Titania.*' Fill in the missing word.

8   Egeus and Hermia are related but how?

9 Match these characters to their professions:

Starveling     Quince     Snug

joiner          carpenter     tailor

10 Who is the Duke of Athens?

11 Flute's first name is Ferdinand. True or false?

12 'Thou art as wise as thou art beautiful.' Who is speaking to whom?

13 Who is King of the Fairies?

14 What is Bottom's profession?

# A Midsummer Night's Dream

1 Who exactly is Hippolyta?

2 Name as many of the mechanicals as you can.

3 Four fairies have names. What are they?

4 'A sweet Athenian lady is in love
   With a disdainful youth;'
Who are they?

5 What is Snout's profession?

6 Identify the two characters in the picture below.

7  He is described as 'a bellows-mender'. Who is he?

8  '*I know a bank where the wild thyme blows,*' A point for every one of the next nine lines you complete.

9  What is Bottom's first name?

10  '*The course of true love never did run smooth*;' Who says this?

11  In how many minutes does Puck say that he will put '*a girdle round about the earth*'?

12  Why have Oberon and Titania quarrelled?

13  Hippolyta talks of a bear hunt with the 'hounds of Sparta'. Where was she when this took place and with whom?

14  Two characters in the play have Robin as their first name. Puck is one. Who is the other?

*A Midsummer Night's Dream*

1 In the Dramatis Personae, how is Philostrate described?

2 Answer the following about the flower that Oberon uses to put juice into Titania's eyes:
(a) What colour was it originally?
(b) What colour is it now?
(c) Why did it change colour?
(d) What is it known as?

3 In the dumb show of Pyramus and Thisbe:
(a) Who plays these two parts?
(b) There are three other named parts. What are they?
(c) Which character speaks the prologue?

4 Identify both the actor and the character in this picture.

5 Connect this picture to the play.

6 Where precisely does Lysander propose to marry Hermia at the beginning of the play?

7 When Oberon and Titania quarrel, who do they accuse each other of being in love with?

8 In Act V, Philostrate offers Theseus a choice of four plays. Pyramus and Thisbe is the one he chooses. Name as many of the others as you can.

9 The following lines are spoken by Puck at the end of the play. Fill in the missing words.
'If we … have …
Think but this, and all is …'

10 We know that Hermia and Helena are different heights. What in the text tells us this?

11 What are Hermia's alternatives if she refuses to marry Demetrius?

12 According to Helena, why is Cupid painted blind?

13 Just before Puck makes the speech beginning 'Now the hungry lion roars' what, according to the stage directions, is he holding?

14 According to Flute, Bottom has the best what 'of any handicraft man in Athens'?

1 Identify the person below and connect him to the play.

2 The clues are New Zealand and Jean Betts. What is the connection?

3 Quote as many lines as you can from Theseus's opening speech.

4 In 2006/7, when the RSC performed all the plays, who directed *A Midsummer Night's Dream* and from which country did the actors come?

5  What is the title of the picture below, and who is the artist?

6  How are Marius Petipa and George Balanchine connected to this play?

7  Who wrote *A Midsummer Night's Gene*?

8  Identify the person below. What is his connection to *A Midsummer Night's Dream*?

# *A Midsummer Night's Dream*

9 Oberon and Puck appear in *A Midwinter Morning's Tale*. What is it and in which series would you find it?

10 Peter Brook's adaptation of *A Midsummer Night's Dream* in 1971 was a landmark. How did he stage it?

11 Name the directors of the 1935 film version, in which Mickey Rooney and James Cagney appeared as Puck and Bottom, respectively.

12 Which two academy awards did this film win?

13 In Peter Hall's 1968 production, name the actresses who played Hermia and Titania.

14 1 June 1960 and Aldebrugh are the clues. What is the answer?

" WHAT ANGEL WAKES ME FROM MY
FLOWERY BED ?"

# *Romeo and Juliet*

1 Name the two warring families.

2 How old is Juliet?

3 *'What's in a name? That which we call a rose*
*By any other name would smell as sweet.'*
Who says this?

4 Which family does Juliet belong to?

5 Tybalt is Montague's nephew. True or false?

6 Who directed the film version shown in the picture (right)?

7 *'But soft! What light through yonder window breaks?'* Who is speaking?

8 Where do Romeo and Juliet first meet?

9 This statue of Juliet is in London. True or false?

10 Benvolio and Tybalt are the first characters on stage, after the chorus. True or false?

11 Where are Romeo and Juliet married and who marries them?

12 Romeo poisons himself. True or false?

13 Complete this line: 'A pair of ... lovers take their life.'

14 Who dies first, Romeo or Juliet?

# *Romeo and Juliet*

1 There are two friars in the play. What are their names?

2 How is Balthasar described in the Dramatis Personae?

3 Who is the Prince of Verona?

4 In the version of *Romeo and Juliet* shown in the picture below, who played the two main roles? What were the names of the two warring factions?

5 What are the final two lines of the play and who speaks them?

6 Capulet thinks that Juliet is too young to marry Paris and asks him to wait but for how many years?

7 Who persuades Romeo to go to the Capulet's party and why?

8 Tybalt has challenged Romeo to a duel. Why?

9  Romeo does not wish to fight Tybalt. What are his reasons?

10  Where exactly would you find this statue?

11  Friar Lawrence's message to Romeo is delayed. Why?

12  Who provides Romeo with poison and in which city?

13  When the play opens, Romeo is in love, but who with?

14  How is this place connected to the play?

# *Romeo and Juliet*

1   Quote as many lines as you can from the prologue.

2   Sampson, Gregory, Peter and Abraham are all servants. Whose servants are they?

3   In the first Act, Romeo reads out a guest list for the Capulet's party. Name as many of the invited guests as you can.

4   What in the text tells us the date of Juliet's birthday and what is that date?

5   When Romeo first sees Juliet, what exactly does he say and to whom?

6   When he meets Juliet herself, what are his first words to her?

7   What exactly is this?

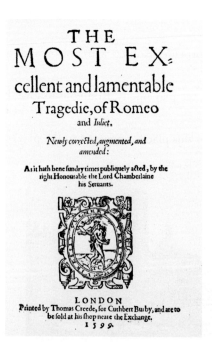

THE
MOST EX:
cellent and lamentable
Tragedie, of Romeo
and *Iuliet*,

*Newly corrected, augmented, and*
*amended*:

As it hath bene sundry times publiquely acted, by the
right Honourable the Lord Chamberlaine
his Seruants.

LONDON
Printed by Thomas Creede, for Cuthbert Burby, and are to
be sold at his shop neare the Exchange,
1 5 9 9.

8  When and where exactly is it arranged that Juliet will marry Paris?

9  Locate exactly where the second prologue occurs.

10  There are five settings in Act II. Name as many as you can.

11  Using this picture, answer the following:
(a) Who is this actress?
(b) Which part did she play
in the 1954 version of *Romeo and Juliet*?

12  What is the format of the prologue?

13  Provide a title for the picture below. This can be in your own words but should be as close as possible to the spirit of the actual title.

# *Romeo and Juliet*

1 How is the person shown below connected to *Romeo and Juliet*?

2 He was born on 29 April 1871 in Russia. Who is he and how is he connected to this play?

3 In 1936, George Cukor directed a version of *Romeo and Juliet*. Why was there criticism of the two actors cast in the leading roles?

4 The film was nominated for four Academy Awards. Name them specifically.

5 What is the earliest known version of the story of *Romeo and Juliet*?

6 Who wrote *The Tragical History of Romeus and Juliet* in 1562, what exactly was it and how is it connected to Shakespeare?

7 *Romeo and Juliet* as robots. What is the film?

8 Connect these clues: D S, *Making Movies*.

9 'And in comes Romeo, he's moaning'. Where would you find this line?

10 Identify the actress shown below and explain her connection and that of her sister Susan to *Romeo and Juliet*.

11 A silent film made in 1908 and filmed in Central Park. What was it?

12 In Quarto 2 iv v 102, what should read as *Enter Peter* reads as what?

13 Sir William Davenant staged a performance of the play in 1662. Who played Romeo?

14 Look at the picture below and identify the artist.

15 Who is shown on this stamp and how is he associated with one of the play's locations?

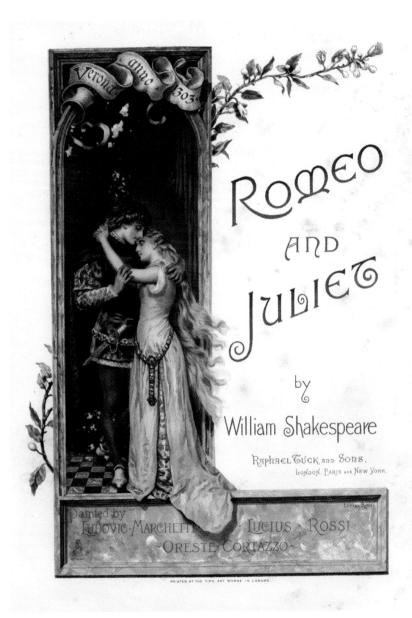

Verona anno 1303

ROMEO
AND
JULIET

by

William Shakespeare

RAPHAEL TUCK AND SONS.
LONDON, PARIS and NEW YORK.

Painted by
LUDOVIC-MARCHETTI - LUCIUS - ROSSI
-ORESTE-CORTAZZO-

LUCIUS ROSSI

PRINTED AT THE FINE ART WORKS IN LONDON.

# *Shakespeare, his Family, his Life and Times*

## EASY

1  Stratford-upon-Avon.
2  He died on 23 April which is assumed to be his birthday.
3  True.
4  (b) Anne.
5  (a) Older.
6  The Bard.
7  Anne Hathaway.
8  Catholic.
9  The sonnets.
10  (a) *Titus Andronicus*;
(b) *Love's Labour's Lost*;
(c) *All's Well That Ends Well*;
(d) *Much Ado About Nothing*.
11  (c) 154.
12  He was one of his brothers.

## MEDIUM

1  The family house in Henley Street.
2  John Shakespeare and Mary Arden.
3  A glover and alderman.
4  National Portrait Gallery, London.
5  John Taylor. The portrait has been attributed to him.
6  King Edward VI Grammar School in Stratford-upon-Avon.
7  It is where his father came from.
8  Actor, writer and part-owner.
9  The Lord Chamberlain's Men. The Lord Chamberlain was their sponsor.
10  Christopher Marlowe.
11  *Venus and Adonis* and *A Lover's Complaint*.

## DIFFICULT

1  26 April 1564.

2  Baptisms took place a few days after birth, so Shakespeare's birth is thought to have been 23 April.

3  These were variations of the spelling of Shakespeare; in Elizabethan times, the spelling of a name was not definitive.

4  Shakespeare would have been able to attend the school without paying because his father was a town official.

5  They are the baptismal dates of Susanna, Shakespeare's first child and his twins, Hanmet and Judith.

6  The late 1580s are known as the 'lost years' (with the period 1578–82 sometimes known as The First Lost Years) because there is no evidence to show where Shakespeare was or why he left Stratford for London.

7  Ben Johnson, playwright, contemporary and friend of Shakespeare.

8  Shakespeare's will.

9  Three of Shakespeare's fellow actors.

10  He was his friend and lawyer.

11  Ben Johnson.

12  Thomas Nash and, on Nash's death, Sir John Bernard.

13  Christopher Marlowe's.

## REQUIRING RESEARCH

1  3 May in the Gregorian calendar was 23 April.

2  Robert Greene.

3  This phrase is a parody of 'Oh, tiger's heart wrapped in a woman's hide' (*Henry The Sixth, Part 3*).

4  *The Phoenix and the Turtle*. Five.

5  Henry Wrothesley, 3rd Earl of Southampton.

6  Edward de Vere, 17th Earl of Oxford; Francis Bacon. They have been suggested as the writers of Shakespeare's plays.

7  Shakespeare's funerary monument is attributed to Gerard Johnson.

8  Nos 138 ('When my love swears she is made of truth') and 144 ('Two loves have I, of comfort and despair'). These two had been published in a 1599 collection called *The Passionate Pilgrim*.

9  (a) The Chandos portrait, named after James Brydges, 1st Duke of Chandos, who owned it. (b) William Davenant was Shakespeare's godson and possibly his illegitimate child.

10  This was the amount Shakespeare left to his friend and lawyer, Francis Collins.

11  Shakespeare and Miguel Cervantes died on the same day.

# *Locations, Buildings and Settings*

## EASY

1 Holy Trinity Church, Stratford-upon-Avon.

2 *Othello* and *The Merchant of Venice*.

3 Shakespeare's house, Stratford-upon-Avon.

4 Two.

5 *The Tempest*.

6 Scotland and England.

7 False. Antony and Cleopatra.

8 Anne Hathaway's.

9 *Windsor*.

10 The Globe Theatre, London.

## MEDIUM

1 Anne Hathaway.

2 Leicester Square, London.

3 *Measure for Measure*.

4 *The First Folio* (1623)

5 Tyre.

6 The Royal Shakespeare Theatre, Stratford-upon-Avon. Elisabeth Scott.

7 *Twelfth Night*.

8 Padua and Petruchio's country house.

9 Holy Trinity Church, Stratford-upon-Avon. Shakespeare's funerary monument.

10 Oliver's house and Frederick's court.

11 Sicilia (Sicily). *The Winter's Tale*.

12 *A Midsummer Night's Dream* and *Timon of Athens*.

# DIFFICULT

1  Navarre. *Love's Labour's Lost*.

2  Edmund, Shakespeare's brother.

3  Germany (Baden).

4  Rousillon, Paris, Florence and Marseilles.

5  (a) Cedar City, Utah (The Adams Theatre) (b) Odessa, Texas (The Globe Theatre of the Great Southwest) (c) San Diego, California.

6  In 1604 or thereabouts, Shakespeare was staying with a family called the Mountjoys who lived north of St Paul's Cathedral.

7  *The Two Gentlemen of Verona, The Merry Wives of Windsor, The Merchant of Venice, Timon of Athens, Hamlet, Prince of Denmark, Othello, The Moor of Venice, Pericles, Prince of Tyre*.

8  Mary Arden's, Shakespeare's mother. Wilmcote, 3 miles northwest of Stratford.

9  *King Henry The Eighth, The Comedy of Errors and Pericles*.

10  Via Capello, 23. The address of the 'Casa di Giulietta'.

11  Near Sardis and near Philippi.

# REQUIRING RESEARCH

1  Bishopsgate, London. The parish of St Helen's.

2  Cyprus, *Othello*. This is the coat of arms for Cyprus.

3  New Place, Stratford-upon-Avon. Hugh Clopton built it and it was the last house Shakespeare lived in.

4  £60. It was the only house in Stratford to be made of brick. (It was also the second largest house in the town.)

5  Blackfriars.

6  Nash's House, which is built on the site of New Place.

7  Rome and the neighbourhood, Corioli and the neighbourhood, and Antrium.

8  Hall's Croft. Susanna, Shakespeare's daughter, and her husband lived there.

9  This sketch (1596) is of a performance on the (thrust) stage of The Swan, which was a typical Elizabethan playhouse, circular and with an open roof.

10  New Place. Francis Gastrell owned the house some time after Shakespeare's death. Angered by the stream of visitors to the house, he destroyed a mulberry tree in the garden, thought to have been planted by Shakespeare. When the people of Stratford broke the windows in retaliation, Gastrell destroyed the house completely.

# Deaths, Ghosts and Gory Bits

## Easy

1  Cleopatra.

2  *Titus Andronicus*.

3  Ophelia.

4  False. She is smothered.

5  She poisons herself with an asp.

6  *King Richard The Third*.

7  Banquo. *Macbeth*.

8  Paris. Romeo has killed Paris in a fight.

9  The witches, Macbeth.

10  He is killed by a poisoned sword.

11  Macduff.

12  True.

13  (c) *King Lear*.

14  Macbeth and Lady Macbeth.

15  Hamlet and the ghost of his father.

## Medium

1  Emilia (*Othello*).

2  Portia (*Julius Caesar*).

3  King Lear and Cordelia.

4  Titus Andronicus.

5  *Antony and Cleopatra*.

6  Antony, Cleopatra, Iras, Charmian, Enobarbus.

7  Titus Andronicus.

8  Macbeth, Duncan's murder.

9  Casca the first, Brutus the last.

10  Tamora, *Titus Andronicus*.

11  Lady Macduff and Fleance.

12  The Earl of Gloucester.

13  *Hamlet*. Claudius has killed Hamlet's father.

14  Brutus is speaking about the ghost of Caesar.

15  Cordelia (*King Lear*).

16  Falstaff.

# Difficult

1 *Othello*. Othello kills Desdemona; Iago kills Emilia.

2 *Measure for Measure*.

3 *Troilus and Cressida*. Troilus is speaking about Hector.

4 Demetrius throws it into a pit.

5 Romeo and Juliet, Lady Macbeth, Ophelia (assumed), Timon of Athens (assumed), Othello, Brutus, Cassius, Portia, Titinius, (*Julius Caesar*) Goneril.

6 The Third Part of *King Henry The Sixth*.

7 Hero, *Much Ado About Nothing*.

8 Aaron (*Titus Andronicus*). Lucius.

9 *Coriolanus*. Aufidius, leader of the Volscians.

10 Timon of Athens.

11 Goneril poisons Regan because of jealousy over Edmund.

12 Desdemona by Delacroix.

13 *King Richard The Second*, Act III, Scene II, 148–164.

14 Lavinia, *Titus Andronicus*.

15 rust; perpetual motion. Falstaff.

# Requiring Research

1 Duke of Clarence (*King Richard III*). Two murderers are sent by Richard to kill him. He is first stabbed and then drowned in a malmsey-butt, a cask of sweet wine.

2 This picture by Titian is of the Duke of Urbino who, in 1538, was murdered by his barber who put a poisoned lotion into his ears. The cause of death of Hamlet's father was based on this real event.

3 Bosworth, the Earl of Richmond, subsequently King Henry VII, kills Richard (*Richard III*).

4 *A Midsummer Night's Dream*.

5 Hotspur.

6 *The Rape of Lucrece*. Lucrece.

7 King John, Hubert.

8 The monk referred to in Question 7. He dies when he tastes King John's food.

9 John Ward, the vicar of Holy Trinity Church in Stratford-upon-Avon.

10 Richard Burbage.

11 (a) Simon Forman
   (b) Doctor and astrologer
   (c) He predicted that he would die on a Thursday night and he did.

12 Marlowe.

# *Who or What is This?*

## EASY

1  A spirit (*The Tempest*).

2  A witch.

3  False. She is in love with Cassio.

4  *Julius Caesar*.

'Of whose true fixed and resting quality

There is no fellow in the firmament.'

5  Bottom.

6  Falstaff.

7  Prospero, *The Tempest*.

8  (a) havoc.

9  Charles, wrestler; Lavache, clown; Dogberry, constable.

10  True.

11  (b) shepherdesses.

12  Hotspur.

1  They are both clowns/jesters.

14  (c) *Venus and Adonis*.

15  They both disguise themselves as men.

## MEDIUM

1  A drunken butler.

2  William.

3  It is the opening line of Sonnet 18.

'Thou art more lovely and more temperate.

Rough winds do shake the darling buds of May,

And summer's lease hath all too short a date:'

4  Roderigo.

5  Imogen. *Cymbeline*.

6  Spirits in *The Tempest*.

7  Costard.

8  viper; breed; husband; father.

9  Painter, jeweller, merchant and mercer.

10  Iago to Othello.

'O, beware, my lord, of jealousy;

It is the green-ey'd monster which doth mock

The meat it feeds on.'

11  Mistress Quickly: *The Merry Wives of Windsor*, Hostess Quickly: *King Henry The Fourth, Parts 1 and 2*; *King Henry The Fifth* (now married to Pistol).

12  The Dark Lady of the Sonnets. This is her first appearance (Sonnet 127).

13  Troilus and Cressida.

14  staff; fathoms; plummet; book.

# DIFFICULT

1 The Parthenon. It was built by Pericles.

2 Assassination, *Macbeth* Act I, Scene VII.

3 Harry the King, Bedford and Exeter, Warwick and Talbot, Salisbury and Gloucester.

4 Antigonus, *The Winter's Tale*.

5 *The Passionate Pilgrim*.

6 Laurence Olivier.

7 'Sometimes a thousand twangling instruments

Will hum about mine ears, and sometime voices

That, if I then had waked after long sleep,

Will make me sleep again: and then, in dreaming,

The clouds methought would open and show riches

Ready to drop upon me that, when I waked,

I cried to dream again.'

8 Title page of the first quarto edition of *Othello*, 1622.

9 Brutus, Cassius, Casca, Trebonius, Ligarius, Decius Brutus, Metellus Cimber and Cinna.

10 skim milk.

11 *The Comedy of Errors*.

12 He is 'gentleman-usher to Queen Katherine.'

13 Desdemona.

14 Moth.

15 Two lords of Tyre (*Pericles*).

# *Who or What is This?*

## REQUIRING RESEARCH

1 Lafeu, an old lord in *All's Well That Ends Well*.

2 Mariana. Tennyson wrote a poem called *Mariana*; a character called Mariana appears both in *Measure for Measure* (one of the problem plays) and in *All's Well That Ends Well*.

3 Michael Radford.

4 Valentine; a character with this name appears in both *Twelfth Night* and *The Two Gentlemen of Verona*.

5 This is a starling and is mentioned in *Henry The Fourth, Part 1*. In 1890, Eugene Scheifflin, who was a fan of Shakespeare, imported starlings from Europe to Central Park in New York, as part of his plan to bring to North America all birds that are mentioned in the plays.

6 zany and madcap: *Love's Labour's Lost*; moonbeam: *A Midsummer Night's Dream*; mountaineer: *Cymbeline*.

7 John Heminges (Hemminge or Hemings). Born in Droitwich Spa, he was an actor and financial manager for the King's Men but is best known as one of the editors of the *First Folio*.

8 1. From a deposition in a court case (1612). 2. Small signature from the seal-ribbon of a conveyance document regarding property in Blackfriars (1613). 3. Small signature from the seal-ribbon of a mortgage document regarding the same property (1613). 4. Decayed small signature from the first page of Shakespeare's will (1616). 5. From the second page of the will. 6. 'By me William Shakspeare' from the third page of the will.

9 Falstaff.

10 Henry Irving, actor, promoted the Beecham Powders poster ('To Beecham or not to Beecham? That is the question.')!

11 *A Lover's Complaint*; unshorn velvet.

12 Christopher Urswick, a priest.

13 Henry Wriothesley, Earl of Southampton and Baron of Tichfield. *The Rape of Lucrece*, which is dedicated to him.

14 *Timon of Athens*; Timon and Flavius.

15 Judith Shakespeare and Susanna Hall.

16 They are the assumed names of Belarius, Guiderius and Arviragus (*Cymbeline*), all of whom are in disguise.

17 Charles Dickens.

18 Sigmund Freud.

# EASY

1 (c) *Love's Labour's Lost.*

2 *Romeo and Juliet.*

3 True.

4 *The Two Gentlemen of Verona.*

5 *King Richard The Third.*

6 True.

7 *Twelfth Night.*

8 *Julius Caesar.*

9 *Hamlet.*

10 *The Merchant of Venice.*

11 Moor.

12 *The Tempest.* (Ariel, Prospero, Ferdinand, Miranda.)

13 (c) *Coriolanus.*

14 *King Henry The Sixth.*

15 *Twelfth Night*, or *What You Will.*

16 (a) *The Winter's Tale.*

17 True.

18 The Prince of Morocco
   *The Merchant of Venice*
   Elbow and Froth
   *Measure for Measure*
   Cloten
   *Cymbeline*

# MEDIUM

1 Helena: *A Midsummer Night's Dream* and *All's Well*; Helen: *Troilus and Cressida* and *Cymbeline*; Helenus: *Troilus and Cressida.*

2 *Othello.*

3 *Coriolanus.*

4 *Twelfth Night.*

5 *The Tempest.*

6 *King Henry The Fifth*; Katherine.

7 *The Merry Wives of Windsor, The First and Second Parts of King Henry The Fourth.*

8 *King Richard The Third.*

9 Pompey: *Measure for Measure*; Launcelot Gobbo: *The Merchant of Venice.*

10 Two: *King Henry The Fourth* and *King Henry The Sixth.*

11 *The Merry Wives of Windsor.*

12 *Macbeth.*

13 *The Taming of the Shrew.*

14 *The Merchant of Venice.*

15 *Much Ado About Nothing.*

# DIFFICULT

1 *Twelfth Night*: Olivia, Viola and Maria; *The Merchant of Venice*: Portia, Nerissa and Jessica.

2 *Measure for Measure.*

3 *Troilus and Cressida.*

4 *King John, King Richard The Second, The First and Second Parts of King Henry The Fourth, King Henry The Fifth, The First, Second and Third Parts of King Henry The Sixth, King Richard The Third, King Henry The Eighth, Hamlet, Prince of Denmark, King Lear, Pericles, Prince of Tyre.*

5 *Julius Caesar, Hamlet, Othello, Timon of Athens, Lear, Macbeth, Antony and*

Cleopatra, Coriolanus.

6  *The Comedy of Errors.*

7  *As You Like It.*

8  *As You Like It*, Jaques. Infant, schoolboy, lover, soldier, justice, pantaloon, second childishness and mere oblivion.

9  *Measure for Measure* and *King John.*

10  *Timon of Athens.*

11  *Antony and Cleopatra.*

12  *Cymbeline.*

13  *Hamlet, Macbeth, Othello, King Lear, Romeo and Juliet, King John, King Richard The Second, King Richard The Third, King Henry The Fifth, King Henry The Fourth (Parts 1 and 2), King Henry The Sixth (Parts 1, 2 and 3), King Henry The Eighth, Troilus and Cressida, Coriolanus, Titus Andronicus, Timon of Athens, Julius Caesar, Antony and Cleopatra, Cymbeline* and *Pericles.*

14  *Measure for Measure.*

15  *King Henry The Eighth.*

16  *As You Like It.*

# REQUIRING RESEARCH

1  Gioachino Rossini who wrote *Otello*, an opera based on *Othello.*

2  This was the date of the first performance of *King Henry The Eighth* when the Globe was burnt to the ground by a fire.

3  *King Lear.* The play was being broadcast on BBC Radio 3 when parts of it were used by John Lennon in the song *I am the Walrus.*

4  Melun: *King John*; Ralph Mouldy: *King Henry The Fourth, Part 2*; Brandon: *King Henry The Eighth.*

5  It is a poster for *Ran*, Akira Kuirosawa's adaptation of *King Lear.*

6  *King Richard The Second.* Bagot is a favourite of the King. Westminster Hall.

7  *A Midsummer Night's Dream, The Merchant of Venice, The Merry Wives of Windsor, Much Ado About Nothing, As You Like It, Richard The Second, Henry The Fourth, Parts 1 and 2, Henry The Fifth, Romeo and Juliet.*

8  Saints Crispin and Crispinian being martyred. The connection is the famous St Crispin Day's speech, which occurs in *King Henry The Fifth.*

9  *Troilus and Cressida.*

10  *King John.*

11  *The Winter's Tale.*

12  *Cymbeline.*

13  Robert Faulconbridge, James Gurney, Constance and Blanch. *King John.*

14  Vaux: *King Henry The Sixth, Part 2*; Fang: *King Henry The Fourth, Part 2*; Sir Stephen Scroop: *King Richard The Second.*

*Hamlet*

## EASY

1 Denmark.
2 Francisco is a soldier; Marcellus is an officer; Fortinbras is the Prince of Norway.
3 True.
4 He is his nephew.
5 (a) at least 26.
6 Ophelia. John William Waterhouse.
7 Ophelia's.
8 Oxford and Cambridge.
9 False. It was July 1602.
10 (c) Marcellus.
11 (c) England.
12 Claudius. By pouring poison into his ear.
13 True.

## MEDIUM

1 (a) I knew him, Horatio. (b) He was the king's jester. (c) fancy; jest.
2 Voltemand, Cornelius, Rosencrantz, Guildenstern and Osric.
3 'To be, or not to be—that is the question;
Whether 'tis nobler in the mind to suffer
The slings and arrows of outrageous fortune,
Or to take arms against a sea of troubles,
And by opposing end them? To die, to sleep—
No more; and by a sleep to say we end
The heart-ache and the thousand natural shocks
That flesh is heir to.—'Tis a consummation
Devoutly to be wish'd. To die, to sleep;
To sleep, perchance to dream. Ay, there's the rub;'
4 The play scene.
5 Tom Stoppard.
6 Ophelia about Hamlet.
7 'friend to Hamlet.'
8 She drinks from a poisoned cup that is intended for Hamlet.
9 Delacroix.
10 Polonius, Claudius and Laertes.
11 It is the play Hamlet arranges to be performed before Claudius and Gertrude.
12 The grave-diggers.
13 Agatha Christie wrote the famously long-running play called *The Mousetrap*; Hamlet tells Claudius that the play which he (Hamlet) arranges to have performed is called *The Mousetrap*.

14  Just over half.

15  Fortinbras.

16  Polonius.

'For loan oft loses both itself and friend,
And borrowing dulls the edge of husbandry.'

# DIFFICULT

1  'Thaw, and resolve itself into a dew!
Or that the Everlasting had not fix'd
His canon 'gainst self-slaughter! O God! God!
How weary, stale, flat, and unprofitable,
Seem to me all the uses of this world!'

2  Crowflowers, nettles, daisies and long purples.

3  In the First Quarto.

4  4,042 lines and 29,551 words.

5  There is a character in it called Ofelia whose father has died.

6  Arthur Rimbaud.

7  Charlie Chaplin.

8  James Joyce.

9  He wrote *I am a Moscow Hamlet*.

10  Coleridge.

11  *A Christmas Carol*.

12  The Third Quarto, 1605. Nicholas Ling who published it.

13  Sam West, Steven Pimlott, 2000.

# REQUIRING RESEARCH

1  There are three texts of *Hamlet*. The First Quarto or Q1 (1603), the Second Quarto or Q2 (1604/05) and the *Hamlet* contained in the First Folio of 1623.

2  He was called Laertes. Laertes is a character in *Hamlet*.

3  Richard Tarleton, an Elizabethan comedian.

4  This was the name for Polonius in the First Quarto.

5  Richard Burbage. The first actor to play the role.

6  Nicholas Rowe and Lewis Theobald. They were early editors of *Hamlet*.

7  Stage directions plus an extra scene.

8  *The Ghost of Elsinor; The Fool in Eden Garden; Odin against Christus; The Serpent in the Orchard.*

9  *Diane Venora*.

10  (a) Innokenty Smoktunovsky; (b) 1964; (c) Grigori Kozintsev

11  (a) Adrian Noble; (b) Ken Branagh and Clifford Rose; (c) Joanne Pearce.

12  Captain William Keeling and crew performed *Hamlet* on board *The Dragon* off Sierra Leone in 1607.

13  Thomas Nashe, 1589. In the introduction he wrote to *Menaphon* by Robert Greene.

14  The *ur-Hamlet* is a lost play, thought to have been in existence in 1589, and a possible source for Shakespeare's play. Thomas Kyd is considered by some to be a possible author of it.

## EASY

1 'When shall we three meet again?'
2 lightning; rain; hurlyburly's; battle's; won.
3 (b) Banquo
4 False.
5 Macduff. Macbeth has been told that 'none of woman born shall harm Macbeth'. Macduff, however, has been born by Caesarian section and therefore can harm him.
6 (c) Reading a letter.
7 False. They are Duncan's.
8 Lady Macbeth.
9 Lady Macbeth.
10 Ian McKellan and Judi Dench.
11 That he will be Thane of Cawdor and King.
12 False. *Macbeth* is the shortest of the tragedies.
13 The Weird Sisters.
14 Harry Potter.
15 The Scottish play.

## MEDIUM

1 As one of the generals in the King's army.
2 Macduff, Lennox, Ross, Menteith, Angus and Caithness.
3 Sinel's.
4 Malcolm to England, Donalbain to Ireland.
5 Jon Finch.
6 Roman Polanski.
7 'Birnam Forest come to Dunsinane.'
8 Norway.
9 'The handle toward my hand? Come, let me clutch thee.
I have thee not, and yet I see thee still.'
10 Macduff and Lennox.
11 The Thane of Cawdor; he was a traitor.
12 It is where Duncan's body is taken; his predecessors are buried there.
13 *Beards*. Macbeth to the witches.
14 A toad.

## DIFFICULT

1 Eye of newt, toe of frog, tongue of dog, sting of blind-worm, leg of lizard and gall of goat.
2 An Armed Head, a bloody child, a crowned child with a tree in his hand.
3 In a restaurant in Glasgow. Macbeth was a chef.

4 Banquo.

5 The King of Norway.

6 A glass. The Stuart line, as a compliment to King James VI of Scotland who had been crowned James I of England when *Macbeth* was written.

7 William Faulkner. The phrase 'full of sound and fury' occurs in Macbeth's speech, Act V, Scene V.

8 Orson Welles.

9 Samuel Taylor Coleridge.

10 *Something Wicked This Way Comes*.

11 Lyndon Johnson.

12 'sides'; 'o'erleaps'.

13 Joshua Reynolds.

14 Neptune's ocean; blood clean; multitudinous incarnadine; green red. Act II.

# REQUIRING RESEARCH

1 He is Giuseppe Verdi, an Italian composer, who wrote the music for the opera *Macbeth* (1847).

2 Because they think there are possible allusions to the gunpowder plot, particularly in the porter's speech.

3 Simon Forman reported seeing the play at the Globe; this is considered to be the earliest account of a performance.

4 Samuel Pepys in his diary of 19 April 1667, commenting on Sir William Davenant's 'operatic' adaption of the play.

5 Leskov wrote *Lady Macbeth of the Mtsensk District* upon which Shostakovich based his opera of the same name.

6 Thomas Middleton, dramatist 1580–1627. It is widely thought that he revised the text of *Macbeth*.

7 Hector Boece or Boyce wrote a historical account of Macbeth of Scotland, and it is thought that Shakespeare used this as the basis of his own play.

8 Mac Bethad mac Findláich c.1005. From 1040 until 1057.

9 Akira Kurosawa. 1957. *Throne of Blood*.

10 *Spider Web Castle*.

11 Fleance speaks the line. John Steinbeck wrote a novel called *The Moon is Down*.

12 Hounds, greyhounds, mongrels, spaniels, curs, shoughs (shaggy dogs), water-rugs (hairy water dogs) and demi-wolves. *Colloquia* by Erasmus.

13 Eugene Ionesco. A French-Romanian playwright and leading figure in the Theatre of the Absurd. He wrote *Macbett*, a satire on *Macbeth*.

## EASY

1 Theseus and Hippolyta's.
2 False. Four days.
3 Hermia, Helena, Hippolyta.
4 Puck.
5 Bottom and Titania.
6 True.
7 *moonlight*.
8 Father and daughter.
9 Starveling is a tailor; Quince is a carpenter; Snug is a joiner.
10 Theseus.
11 False. Francis.
12 Titania to Bottom.
13 Oberon.
14 Weaver.

## MEDIUM

1 Queen of the Amazons.
2 Quince, Bottom, Snug, Flute, Snout, Starveling.
3 Peaseblossom, Moth, Cobweb, Mustardseed.
4 Helena and Demetrius.
5 Tinker.
6 Pyramus and Thisbe.
7 Flute.
8 'Where oxlips and the nodding violet grows,
Quite over-canopied with luscious woodbine,
With sweet musk-roses and with eglantine;
There sleeps Titania sometime of the night,
Lull'd in these flowers with dances and delight;
And there the snake throws her enamell'd skin,
Weed wide enough to wrap a fairy in;
And with the juice of this I'll streak her eyes,
And make her full of hateful fantasies.'
9 Nick.
10 Lysander.
11 Forty.
12 Oberon wants to have as his 'henchman' the small boy whose mother has died and who Titania is now raising.
13 A wood in Crete, with Hercules and Cadmus.
14 Starveling, the tailor.

## DIFFICULT

1  Master of the Revels to Theseus.
2  (a) White; (b) Purple; (c) Cupid's bolt fell on it; (d) Live-in-idleness.
3  (a) Bottom plays Pyramus and Flute plays Thisbe; (b) Wall, Moonshine and Lion; (c) Quince.
4  Anthony Quale, Bottom.
5  This is Titania, the fourteenth and largest of Uranus's known satellites.
6  At his widow aunt's house, seven leagues from Athens.
7  Theseus and Hippolyta.
8  'The battle with the Centaurs, to be sung/ By an Athenian eunuch to the harp.'
'The riot of the tipsy Bacchanals, /Tearing the Thracian singer in their rage.'
'The thrice three Muses mourning for the death/Of Learning, late deceas'd in beggary.'
9  shadows; offended; mended.
10  Act III, Scene 2: Helena calls Hermia 'you puppet' which Hermia takes as a reference to her height. She goes on to say that Helena has 'a tall personage' and that she, Hermia, is 'so dwarfish and so low'.
11  'to die the death, or to abjure For ever the society of men.'
12  Because love 'looks not with the eyes, but with the mind;' Act I, Scene I.
13  A broom.
14  Wit.

## REQUIRING RESEARCH

1  Felix Mendelssohn, composer. He composed an overture and incidental music for *A Midsummer Night's Dream*.
2  Jean Betts, a New Zealand playwright, wrote *Revenge of the Amazons* as a feminist version of *A Midsummer Night's Dream*.
3  'Now, fair Hippolyta, our nuptial hour
Draws on apace; four happy days bring in
Another moon; but, O, methinks, how slow
This old moon wanes! She lingers my desires,
Like to a step-dame or a dowager,
Long withering out a young man's revenue.'
4  Tim Supple. India.
5  *The Quarrel of Oberon and Titania*, Joseph Noel Paton.
6  Both adapted it for the ballet.
7  Andrew Harman.
8  Orson Scott Card. He wrote *Magic Street* in which the Bag Man is Puck.
9  A comic in the Corto Maltese series by Hugh Pratt.
10  In a white box.
11  Max Reinhardt and William Dieterle.
12  Best cinematography and best film editing.
13  Helen Mirren and Judi Dench.
14  This was the premiere of Benjamin Britten's opera of the play.

# *Romeo and Juliet*

## EASY

1 The Montagues and the Capulets.
2 She is not yet fourteen.
3 Juliet.
4 The Capulets.
5 False. He is Lady Capulet's nephew.
6 Franco Zeffirelli.
7 Romeo.
8 At a masked party at the Capulet's house.
9 False. It is in Verona.
10 False. Sampson and Gregory.
11 They are married by Friar Lawrence in his cell.
12 True.
13 star-cross'd
14 Romeo.

## MEDIUM

1 Friar Lawrence and Friar John.
2 As 'servant to Romeo'.
3 Escalus.
4 Natalie Wood and Richard Beymer. The Jets and the Sharks.
5 'For never was a story of more woe
Than this of Juliet and her Romeo.'
Spoken by Escalus.
6 Two.
7 Benvolio because Rosaline will be there.
8 He is angry because Romeo has been to the Capulet's house.
9 Romeo is now married to Juliet and does not want to fight her cousin (Tybalt).
10 New York.
11 The message is sent via Friar John who is put into quarantine.
12 An apothecary in Mantua.
13 Rosaline.
14 It is Mantua, which is a setting in *Romeo and Juliet*.

# DIFFICULT

1 'Two households, both alike in dignity,
In fair Verona, where we lay our scene,
From ancient grudge break to new mutiny,
Where civil blood makes civil hands unclean.
From forth the fatal loins of these two foes
A pair of star-cross'd lovers take their life;
Whose misadventured piteous overthrows
Doth with their death bury their parents' strife.
The fearful passage of their death-mark'd love,
And the continuance of their parents' rage,
Which, but their children's end, nought could remove,
Is now the two hours' traffic of our stage;
The which if you with patient ears attend,
What here shall miss, our toil shall strive to mend.'

2 Sampson and Gregory are the Capulet's servants; Peter is the nurse's servant; Abraham is the Montague's servant.

3 'Signior Martino and his wife and daughters; County Anselme and his beauteous sisters; the lady widow of Vitruvio; Signior Placentio and his lovely nieces; Mercutio and his brother Valentine; mine uncle Capulet, his wife and daughters; my fair niece Rosaline and Livia; Signior Valentio and his cousin Tybalt, Lucio and the lively Helena.'

4 'Come Lammas Eve at night shall she be fourteen.' Lammas is 1 August, therefore her birthday is 31 July.

5 'What lady's that which doth enrich the hand Of yonder knight?'
He is speaking to a servant.

6 'If I profane with my unworthiest hand This holy shrine, the gentle fine is this:'

7 Title page of the Second Quarto of Romeo and Juliet (published 1599).

8 On Thursday morning at St Peter's Church.

9 At the start of Act Two.

10 A lane by the wall of Capulet's orchard; Capulet's orchard; Friar Lawrence's cell; A street; Capulet's orchard.

11 (a) Flora Robson, (b) the nurse.

12 It contains fourteen lines and is in the form of a Shakespearean sonnet.

13 *The Reconciliation of the Montagues and Capulets.*

# Requiring Research

1 Leonard Bernstein. He wrote the music for *West Side Story*.

2 Sergei Prokoviev. He wrote the music for a ballet, *Romeo and Juliet*.

3 Leslie Howard and Norma Shearer were older than teenagers.

4 Best Picture, Best Supporting Actor, Best Actress, Best Art Direction.

5 1476; *Mariotta and Gianozzo of Siena* by Masuccio Salernitano.

6 Arthur Brooke; it is a narrative poem and Shakespeare used it as a source for his play.

7 *Romie-0 and Julie-8* (also known as *Runaway Robots!*).

8 Dire Straits recorded the album *Making Movies*, which included the song *Romeo and Juliet*.

9 *Desolation Row* by Bob Dylan from the album *Highway 61* revisited.

10 Charlotte Saunders Cushman and her sister Susan famously took the parts of Romeo and Juliet in an 1845 version of the play in America.

11 The first American film version of *Romeo and Juliet*.

12 *Enter Will Kempe*.

13 Henry Harris.

14 Ford Maddox Brown.

15 This is Virgil (Publius Virgilius Maro). He was born near Mantua.

## Acknowledgements

National Archives (www.nationalarchives.gov.uk), page 15 (top).
Royal Shakespeare Company archives, pages 54, 60, 61 (top), 74 (bottom), 77 (top and right), 90 and 92 (right).